DIVINE GUIDANCE OR JUST PLAIN HAPPENSTANCE

John K Probst

CONTENTS

Title Page

PREFACE   1

CHAPTER 1:   2
A CHILD'S CURIOSITY

CHAPTER 2:   6
FROM A SANDWICH COUNTER TO A NAME ENCOUNTER

CHAPTER 3:   13
A ROOM RENTERS REMINISCENSE AND REUNION

CHAPTER 4:   17
THE PREDESTINED PAINTING OF A FAMILIAR PORTRAIT

CHAPTER 5:   19
MOBILITY WITH A MIND OF ITS OWN

PREFACE

Four unusual instances occurred within my growing years that I neither intentionally contemplated, planned, or consciously conceived. These instances stand out as unusual happenings, because there were no preplanned motives on my part for their eventual positive outcomes.

These instances occurred and resolved not by some divine direction, but by pure unadulterated happenstance. To this day I have these occurrences in my mind's memory with such specificity, that they very well might have happened yesterday. Why these instances occurred and were positively resolved I do not know, and so leave it up the reader of this novel to come to his or her own conclusions. Readers, are these stories and their final occurrences and positive resolutions, evolved by divine guidance or just plain happenstance. I will let you decide.

CHAPTER 1:
A CHILD'S CURIOSITY

I was just four years old when, on that sunny afternoon, my mother placed me on the front lawn of our home to play and run within the fenced in front lawn. When left, the phone rang and she said, "now you play here" and proceeded to enter the house to answer the ringing phone. Left momentarily, I looked about and realized not only was I alone, but the fence gate exiting the front lawn was open. Hearing her converse on the phone I knew she would not soon return, and so, taking advantage of the opened gate proceeded to leave the yard, run down the stair and onto the cement walk in front of the house.

Once there, I could still hear my mother's voice inside the house and looking to what I was told was my front, could see the trees and their hanging limbs making a sort of tunnel. The view was so interesting that I wanted to immediately run into that tunnel and see where it ended. Still hearing my mother's voice in the house, I decided to run toward the hanging tunnel of leaves and branches before she returned to the porch. Running as fast as I could, I knew I should not be on the sidewalk, but being so curious about the tunnel, I just hoped she would not miss me.

Upon running halfway towards my designated destination, I slowed down, then walked, then stopped. Phew! I was breathing heavily but was assured I was out of sight when my mother would return to the porch. Slowly I walked to the end of the cement walk and then stopped. I thought back on trips I had taken with my grandfather in his car. He would stop at this same intersection of the two streets and say, "This is Polk Street "and then poke me in the ribs. I in turn would poke him and then we would both have good laugh. From previous rides, I knew that he turned to what I knew to be my left, then travel a few minutes, and turn to what I knew to be my right and soon we would park at my grandmother's front door.

I had all the intention of follow the same procedural directions but then realized I was next to an empty lot with a well-worn path sided by weeds as erect and straight as I was tall. But this observation took me in opposition to my intended direction. Walking onto the path, I enjoyed being surrounded by the overgrowth and when the path ended, I looked back. This was not the direction I had intended, and was about to turn to my left side, when I noticed that down the street there were iron tracks.

As I watched, a train on the tracks came into view. Hey! I had a wooden train just like that as a present from Santa Clause at Christmas time. Now I wanted to see what a real train on metal tracks looked like, and so began walking down the new (Polk) street toward the tracks. When arriving at the tracks, no train was in sight, and so I decided to follow the rails in the direction I had seen the train move. After what was several blocks, the houses along the way ended and I found myself amongst empty lots of high weeds all around me.

Seeing the train coming in my direction, I got off the metal rails and backed into a weeded empty lot. As the train passed me, I waved to the people inside, and they waved back to me. (As an adult remembering the occasion, I wondered why none of the passengers ever wondered what a four-year standing alone, was doing waving at them from an empty field without some kind of accompanied adult supervision.) After the train passed, I looked across the wide road and saw a paved alley way sided by tall trees whose limbs and leave encircled the area like a tunnel and again, I was curious to see where that tunnel might end.

Crossing the wide street, I entered the alley and proceeded to walk along until the empty lots turned into houses garages and back yards. And to my utter surprise, to my left, one of the back yards just seemed to appear from nowhere, and I recognized it immediately as my grandmas back yard. And there in the yard where the swings and slide my grandparents had bought for me to play with when visiting them. Immediately, I entered the yard and climbed onto one of the swings.

From my position I could see my grandfather leaving the front of the house, and so wanting to gain his attention, I got off the swing and called to him, but by then, he had gotten into his car and drove away. I returned to my swing and within minutes my grandma appeared at the back door and said, "Oh! That silly old man, he didn't tell me he had dropped you off. You come right in here, Nannie, has some rice pudding for you." Hungry and tired, I was more than willing to oblige.

While eating my rice pudding and conversing with my grandma, I heard my grandfather's car stop out front. "I'm going to have a word with him," said my grandmother. He came into the house and straight into the kitchen. As my grandma began to scold him for not telling her he had dropped me off, he suddenly reached over, picked me up and said,

"Mae (my mother) wants to see him right know. As my grandma yelled, but you just left him here! He said nothing and we left. He then placed me in his car, and he drove to my house. Upon arriving I remembered seeing two black police cars with their red lights on the side and another on the roof. My mother and dad stood in the front yard directing a troop of uniformed boy scouts, and others as to where to look to find me.

"I've got him here "yelled my grandfather as he picked me up and we ran toward my mother. My mother grabbed me and hugged me and then turned and took me into the house. She stripped me to make sure I was not in any way hurt, and then said, "you're going right to bed." Being tired from my long walk I was glad to lay down. She stayed with me at my bed side until I was soon fast asleep.

As an adult I told relatives and friends of my adventure. My mother and grandmother had a hard time believing that I had walked that far and had by happenstance just happened to come across my grandmother's backyard. My mother believed that I might have been picked up by a stranger then for some reason, released at my grandmother's house.

My father said, "Hey, if someone kidnapped him for ransom they picked the wrong kid,---- I don't have any money."

As stated,----- to this day, I remember my four-year-old adventure as though it happened just yesterday!

CHAPTER 2:
FROM A SANDWICH COUNTER TO A NAME ENCOUNTER

Upon graduating from high school, I had no special plans for the summer months before beginning my college career. The uncomfortable summer heat and no local plans pressured me into considering the possibility of finding work in Chicago, which was 90 miles around the base of Lake Michigan. The more I thought if the possibility the more I wanted to make it a reality. And so, once I made up my mind, I told my mother.

"Oh! Jake, what do you want to do a thing like that? Chicago is just as hot, or even hotter than here, and …. Well, it is not the safest place to be in. Why don't you just stay here, there's plenty to do at the farm."

"Mom"! I reiterated, "staying at the farm, cleaning out the barns and raking the front yard, while having nowhere else to go for three months just does not interest me." "I understand, "she sighed, "but I will worry about you, and you must promise to call me every so often, so I know you are safe and well."

I promised that I would keep in contact. And so, with everything 'squared away' at home, I packed a bag, and climbed on the South Shore train that would take me straight into the Chicago business district better known as the Chicago Loop. Upon arriving I knew that there were cheap rooms available at the YMCA on lower Randolph Street. Leaving the train station, I took a bus to the "Y" and got a single room for the very reasonable price of nine dollars a week or thirty-five for an entire month. I then set out to find a salaried position.

Walking up Randolph Street, my minds memory took me to another time and younger age. I was only ten years old, when my grandma had taken me down this very street. We stopped in front of one of the large entrance doors. "See that floor" she said," I paid over $10,000 in 1920 to upgrade the restaurant, called the Gen Inn, I was managing then. Well, it never paid off, but at least it looked professional." Looking at the various buildings to my right I could not remember which building floor she had referred to.

Upon reaching the "Y" I registered for a room and plunked down $35.00 for a full month's rent. Then determined to find employment went back up Randolph Street. Three blocks up and in the corner of the window of the Chandler Restaurant a small sign read- sandwich counter clerk position available. Upon entering I was instructed to go to a Mr. Kneely's office on the second floor.

Entering his office, I told a secretary of my interest in the position.

"Here, take this paper, sit there and fill it out. Be sure to enter a phone number or place where we can contact you." I filled out all the necessary information about myself and my "Y" address. When finished, the secretary viewed the contents and said,

"Thank you, Mr. Jake Philips? I nodded yes, and then she said, Mr. Mr. Kneely will take this into consideration."

I left the office and decided to walk around my new surroundings. Each building seemed bigger than the last one viewed. And my mother was right, Chicago was just as hot, if not hotter, than it was in my hometown. Upon arising the next morning, I went to the main "Y"s desk in the lobby. And to my surprise I was given a note from the Chandler Restaurant Organization signed by a Mr. Kneely. He instructed me to come straight to his office for possible employment.

"Wow!" I said to myself that was quick. I didn't expect to hear from any possible employer for weeks and had decided that if I could not find employment, I was ready to return home to clean those barns and rake that lawn.

Upon entering his office, his secretary told me to wait; that he would be with me with in a moment. And to her word, a moment later, out walked a thin small neatly dressed individual whose speech patterns, gestures and nervous twitches would earn him the well-deserved name of Nervous Kneely. From the moment he moved talked, or gestured, he was a 'nervous nelly type" if ever I saw one.

"OH! ...OH!.. yes ..yes.. you are...let me see...yes...you are Jake Philips...just as ..it says here....yes.. yes...and you looking of the service counter...position right?...yes..yes... that is... what you..have ..yes ..written.

Before I could reply he said,

"Well.. I have shown your application along with the ...the many others, we ....that is..that is.. that.. I .....received, yes..., and.. ...and ...yes...yes. Mr. Chandler insisted.. ...yes ...he insisted.. that...yes... yes..yes that I choose you! I will tell you.... Yes I was .. I was....surprised.....yes...But ..Mr.. Mr. Chandler is the Operational Chief and President and... what...what.. he says.... What he says... we do... He then he let out a little nervous chuckle. The guy's movements, dialogue and gestures were exhausting to listen and watch. With such a persona, he must be exhausted at the end of the day.

"You start ... tomorrow, at one pm and work till six pm. At two dollars an hour. And.. and..you..you get to keep..all .all your tips.

Is that...that..fully agreed...agreed ..upon by..by you?

Tomorrrow, you..you will have to show ..show up ten minutes... yes..ten minutes early.. I have to..have to show you. How we..how to make the sandwiches with . without touching..without..touching them. That procedure is..yes..is one of our ..our specialties... in this ..this organization. And Oh yes!...yes. be sure to wear. .to wear a clean..... white...... shirt.

Upon leaving his office, I wondered if listening and watching the man's gyrations, agitation s and nervous gestures were contagious. Anyway, I figured it was worth the challenge to keep the position.

And then I thought back on what he had said about choosing my application. What was it, Oh yes!, 'A Mr. Chandler had specifically told old Nervous Kneely that I should gain the position?' I could not figure what I could have possibly written on the application to gain that kind of affirmation, but hey, I was glad to get the work. I now had a place of employment and residence, and they were within several blocks of each other and on the same street. Hmmm! I thought that should make my mom more comfortable with my move.

Upon rising, I ate a short breakfast of coffee and a roll, then put on a clean white shirt, and slowly walked up Randolph Street. Arriving at 12: 50, I went to Mr. Keely's office. He then escorted me to a side counter to demonstrate how just to make a sandwich in front of a hungry customer. With a wide sharp kitchen knife in one hand, and a cooks two prone fork in the other, he picked out the lettuce, onion, and tomato, while holding each with the fork, he slicked each and placed them on bead that he had buttered with mayonnaise. Having constructed the sandwich, he placed the large knife under the plate holding the sandwich and placed it up onto the counter. "And that my good man is how ...is how.. one makes a sandwich in...in.. this establishment without ever touching...touching the ingratiates. Now you do it!

On my first try I got all the ingredients cut and into a sandwich, and the sandwich on to the plater, but upon lifting the plate and its contents onto the counter, I misplaced the position of the knife, and all the ingredients flipped into the air and all over the floor and counter.

"I will leave you here with the ingredients, and when...when.. you feel you have accomplished the task correctly, contact me and….and I will you put up….up…. on the far end of the counter."

As he walked away, I thought, He had not fired me, or inferred in any way, that I would be dismissed or fired while learning the sandwich making process, in fact, while thinking back on what he had said, remembered him saying, he was distinctly instructed to hire me. This seemed to be a mystery to me but then I thought maybe "Hey I am just making something out of nothing."

After accomplishing the sandwich making task, Mr. Kneely went over the menu, the prices and told me to always return any change correctly with the largest of bills and/or change. "And don't forget…forget.. to smile!"

Now a sandwich and coffee tea or milk, the average order, came to 90 cents. And the customer usually placed a single dollar on the counter, and said, " keep the change" and so after a 6-hour workday, we servers left with a pocket full of dimes.

During my third week at the counter, I was busy making a customer's sandwich, when Nervous Kneely approached me and said. "Finish that sandwich and then come to my office." Upon finishing my work, I did as he instructed. Upon entering he stood up and said, "come in and shut the door." I had just closed the door, and when he said, "I don't know what you said or did that …that ..has caused this..this incident, but I have ..I have,,,instructions..instructions from Mr. Chandlers office to take you…yes..you to him immediately. Did..did you do..do something..say something…why is he so insistent…you..you must have done . done. something!"

I insisted that I had not said or had done anything that might have offended a customer, but Mr. Kneely continue. " You must have said something or did something to cause this!! No one ..no one… of the servers have ever been taken…ever taken…. for any reason to Mr. …Mr. Chandlers private office. "You must have done …done ..something…….something.!!!!

Upon exiting the elevator, the room before us was used definitely for business organizational purposes. In the center was a long table surrounded by several chairs. At the far end was a door to an office, and from it came a Miss Stephens, Mr. Chandlers secretary.

"Mr. Keely, your services will not be needed, and you may return to your office." Upon her demand, his eyes bugged out because he was disappointed that he would not be present at the meeting. As he left, he looked at me as though to say, 'behave yourself!'

"Mr. Jacobs, if you will please come into Mr. Chandlers office." She opened the door, and a very large middle-aged man sat at his desk signing papers.

Miss Stephens moved by the side of his desk and picked up all the papers he had signed. When he had finished, he placed the pen at his side, then told her to please close the door on her way out. As I sat down, he took several papers, moved them to the out box, then put the caps back on the pens, and folding his hands in front of himself he turned to me and said,

"How's your grandmother?"

Taken completely by surprised I said, " She is fine. I think she is in Florida, but I know she will be visiting us when she comes north."

"Well, when you see her, you tell her Joe Chandler said hello and when in Chicago, to drop by."

Still taken back, I said, "You know my grandma?"

"Know her! Why we have been friends for 30 years. It was she that came by when I first opened this restaurant, and wished me as a competitor, the best of luck. There is a picture of her, me, and my brother George over there on the wall."

Upon viewing the portrait, I saw a woman, 30 years younger resembling my grandma holding a bottle of campaign. Behind her were two men. All had big smiles on their faces. "When I was in my cups, as they say, it was your grandma who picked me up and demanded that I go with her to weekly Alcoholic Anonymous meetings My brother George never went. Because of his drinking, he died many years ago. Ya know, in sense I owe my life to your grandma for encouraging me to sober up. I haven't had a drink in 20 years."

"How did you know I was her grandson?"

"I have only known one man named Jacob K. Philips in my life, and when viewing your work application, I knew you were her favorite grandson, and the child named after her husband She referred to you as her piano playing little grandson. Do you still play?" Still gazing at the portrait, I said, "yes, in fact I am majoring in music at the university."

Standing up he said, "well thank you for coming in, and be sure to tell your grandma when in Chicago to drop by."

Shaking hands, I said I would not forget and excused myself.

I left the room and entered the elevator still amazed at what had just transpired. When the elevator stopped and I got out, there stood Mr. Keely.

"What...what...did...did he say...what happened, did he mention...mention my name ..... I mean...why....why did he...why did he... want to..to...see...to see.. you?"

I smiled and looked coyly and curiously at Mr. Keely and then in a very soft voice said, "Mr. Keely, he never mentioned your name, or my conduct with any of the customers. And as for my meeting with Mr. Chandler well....you see,........... we go............we go..... Hmmm....how should I put it.....Oh ya.....we go......... waaaaaay back!!!!!!

CHAPTER 3:
A ROOM RENTERS
REMINISCENSE
AND REUNION

After having driven over 150 miles I eventually arrived in downtown San Francisco. The sun was setting, I was tired, and wanted nothing more than to get out of the car, get something to eat and fall asleep in a nice soft bed. Being new to my surroundings, I decided to take the first turn off from the freeway. A sign ahead read 7th Street. That was good enough for me, and so I turned down the off ramp on to 7th street exit, and into the parking lot of the 7th Street Motel. Upon entering the office, I signed for a room costing $7.00 a night. Seven dollars at the Seven Street Motel. These facilities would temporarily do, but I realized I would have to find accommodations more in line with my dwindling money supply.

I ate at a diner down the block and realized my surroundings were not in the best part of town. Twice, intoxicated street beggars asked if I had any change, I wanted to get rid of. Upon entering my room, and without even shutting off the light, I fell fast asleep. Upon awakening, I realized I had an hour before signing out, and while lying in bed decided my first task was to find cheaper living facilities. Greeting the on-coming day, I dressed, returned to the 'dive-like' diner, ate a roll and digested it with an accompanying cup of coffee.

Upon returning to the motel, I packed my bag, signed out and received directions for a residential part of the city that might have rentals. I eventually found myself on Sacramento St. On both sides of the street were businesses and boarding houses. Seeing a sign in front of one of the renting facilities that read $65.00 a month, I decided this was about as good as it was going to get. And so, exiting the car I walked up to the entrance and knocked. No one answered and then a car pulled up and a woman with packages in her arms got out. Besides juggling the packages, her imbalance was evidence that she had had something to drink.

"What do you want?" "I'm looking for a place to rent. Can I help you with those packages?" Saying yes, we went into building and placed the packages on a table in the hallway. "Is there just you renting or other persons" she asked. "Just me," I answered. She squinted her eyes as she gazed with caution and suspicion at me. "I don't usually rent to guys, especially single guys, the last one got drunk all the time and had parties and caused all sorts of a confrontations with my other tenants. Ehhh! I don't. know."

"Look", I said, on my defense, "I am new to the area, I don't know anyone, and will promise that I won't have wild parties or any other disturbances that will upset you or your other tenants. In silence she sobered up a bit and I knew she wanted the rental money and was considering taking a chance on me. "I can get references if you want." Still glaring at me she said. "Let me show you the rooms" Opening the apartment door, I saw a small living room, with a pint-sized refrigerator in the corner beside a two-burner electric appliance. To the left was a door that opened into a bedroom. Inside was a double bed and small dresser. To the left of the bed was another door.

"That door goes into the bathroom facility that you share with the other tenants on this floor. When using the facility, lock that door leading to the hallway, and when leaving, be sure to unlock that hallway door, then when entering your bedroom, lock your door so you won't be disturbed."

It was obvious from what she said that she was considering the possibility of renting me the apartment.

As she picked up the packages she looked suspiciously at me again, and then said, Eeh!! I don't know."

Realizing I was losing her confidence I quickly replied, "Look my name is Jacob Philips, I just arrived here from my home town in Middle land Indiana and……

That is as far as I got. She slowly put down the packages, turned to me and still squinting said. "What did you say?" Repeating I said, my name is Jacob Philips from Middletown Indiana and I …

OH MY GOD!!!! She screamed and running towards me, wrapped her hands around my neck and with her intoxicating breath yelled YOU ARE THE LITTLE NEPHEW THAT PLAYS PIANO.!!!

Releasing myself from her grasp, I said" What do you mean. What are you talking about"?

OH!... my dear boy, I am an old friend of your Aunt Rose. She and I were friends thirty years ago in this very town. She told me about you and how she would accompany you on the piano while at your young age of five, you would play nursery rhyme songs like..ah?.. Mary had a little lamb. OHHH!! Of course, you can rent the rooms. OHHH!! Wait till I tell my friends and I will surely call her and announce who my new tenant is.

A month or so later, my Aunt Rose came to town and since I had a car, I chauffeured the two ladies to museums, musical shows, touring spots and evening dinners as they talked about the old days and since then, what had transpired in their lives.

With the ladies paying the entrance fees, dinner tips and checks, I ate at some very expensive restaurants. I saw stage productions I could not have afforded to view, and in the process, learned how to maneuver those highly hilly highways and byways of San Francisco streets.

The following month I went up to her apartment to pay my rent. I knocked on the door and heard, "Ya…come..come… on..on..in."

She was obviously very drunk. She stood there in a tight fitting and revealing robe.

"Hey!... you wouldn't be interested in a glass of wine would you..? I mean….. We could get better acquainted. …If …. Yaa know what …what I mean?"

I wasn't interested and said, "no thank you", then placed my check on a table and left thinking, "Wow, I just got an offer to be a toy boy from my landlady."

When phoning my dad, I told him who my landlady was. Recognizing her name he said, "You mean to say that you drove over 2000 miles to rent a room from a woman who is your Aunt Rose's old friend. Of all the possible rentals in San Francisco, what are the odds of that happening? I guess that might mean you were destined to go west."

CHAPTER 4:
THE PREDESTINED
PAINTING OF A
FAMILIAR PORTRAIT

As Drama Director at the college, I was in the middle of directing the play, "The Prime Of Miss Brodie", a play about Jean Brodie, a

ego centered women who always had alternative motives for her actions. Within the play an artist falls in love with her, and in the play directions he shows her a two by four ft previously painted portrait of a man and says, "Just think of what I can do for your portrait"

For this scene I needed a two by four ft canvas prop of a portrait of a man from the should line up. My neighbor at the time made her living painting portraits of individuals, and so asked her if she could paint a portrait of a man on a 2ft by 4 ft canvass. She said "yes". We agreed on a price and until I received it, we used an equivalent size piece of carboard. But the gentleman playing the part of Miss Brodie's lover, would challenge his female counterpart's sense of humor by putting various silly messages on the bare front of the cardboard.

He would pull out the board, she would view it and on it would be written "Roses are red violets are blue, you can't see me, but I can see you! Or "Felicitations and various calculations can cause undo sweat and additional perspirations!" Before the end of this serious scene both would be laughing and break the dramatic moment. And so, I was very happy to receive the final portrait which the artist had wrapped in a covering. But when I took off the cover I could not believe what I saw.

"WOW! what did you use for a model" I asked "Just a picture of a man I got out of some magazine. I needed it to determine proportions for the larger dimensions why?" "Because my dear, you have painted an exact portrait of my grandfather as I remember him when I was 7 years old."

"WHAT" "You heard me, this portrait is of my grandfather, my mother's dad, as I remember him. He died when I was 7 years old."

Surprised and feeling almost guilty she said, "Well.. Jake,…. I did 't mean to,…. I mean….. I mean………, hey! This is crazy…. I've never seen a picture of your grandfather, I just painted what was in my minds 'eye'." " Well, your minds eye must have been working overtime because that portrait is of my grandpa Jake Philips of whom I am named after.

When the run of the play ended, instead of me putting the portrait in the prop closet, I took it home, and from then, to this very day, it has held a prominent place on my bedroom wall.

CHAPTER 5:
MOBILITY WITH A
MIND OF ITS OWN

I had only been in the San Francisco area for a few months when I remembered having met a San Francisco resident while in the army. Joe

Sheldon was his name, and he had always said, *"Hey! if you come to S.F., drop in for a visit and try out my mom's great cooking."* Finding his phone number, I called Joe up, and sure enough, I was invited to a Sunday brunch at his place, which was at the top of Fenton St. *"Just Park anywhere on Fenton and look up the hill. You will see some idiot waving his hand at you, that is me.* Following his directions, one sunny Sunday afternoon, I drove to Fenton St. parked the car at the top of the street that stretched down at least three blocks long and ended at an intersection. Getting out of the car, I looked up the hill, and high from an apartment window, a guy was waving at me. Taking one last look at the car, I made sure the tires were pointed toward the curve, a lawful requirement of any down grade parking in the town.

For the next three hours we ate his mom's delicious roast beef dinner and apple pie dessert, while we talked about various incidences during our army active duty. Realizing the lateness of the hour, I excused myself, said my goodbye, and headed toward Fenton St. When reaching the top, I began to question, just where I had parked. Looking down the long street, I realized why I could not find my car. It was now parked at the bottom of the hill and up against a large tree that had stopped it from moving further. A police officer reached into the car, opened the driver's side door and was taking down the license number. Running down the hill my only thought on the matter was, that someone had tried to steal my car. Approaching the officer I said, *"Did someone try to take the car"*? The officer looked up from his writing and said, in a very ominous tone,

"Oh no sir, it got down here all by itself. "I knew then that I was in big trouble!

"By itself?" I asked. And he said, *"By itself, and I have witness to prove it."*

At this point in the story telling, I must digress and describe my car. It was an automatic drive 1948 red Chevy that I had bought months before from a musical colleague. The engine parts were, to put in a charitable word, "loose" and so I got about 10 miles to the gallon, and it needed a new quart of oil engine every 3-400 miles of travel. Much to the surprise of my parents and friends, it had taken me from the Mid-West to San Francesco without incident. HMMM!!! And now this! The lever the driver pulled to put the brakes on all the tires, pulled up as though the brakes were completely stilled, but in reality, nothing happened. Some metal piece that pulled the brakes into place shirred off and thus when pulling on the brake lever, it only gave the impression that the brakes were placed against the tire drums.

"This is your car" the officer asked. "yes" I replied. *"May I see your driver's license.?"*

While he wrote down the license information, I said, *"I don't understand."* He looked up at me, and said,

"According to what witnesses have said, your car, probably from being bumped from behind, turned its wheels from the curb to the road, then it slowly moved out to the middle of the street, and without crashing into any other car or hitting the children playing in the street, it rolled downward. At this position where there was no car parked, it turned

to the right and drove into this tree. Fortunately, the tree stopped the vehicle from traveling farther and hitting the glass plating on the side of grocery store two feet away. I am writing you a ticket for vehicular endangerment, that means that you will have to appear before a judge. You have a right to represent yourself or bring your own counsel. If you cannot afford counsel, a representative will be made available for you. Do you have any questions? "I answered "no" . Then he said, "mister, you have the luck of the Irish or some kind of divine guidance. Signing his name at the bottom, He gave me the ticket and drove off.

In my mind's eye, I visioned my car being bumped, causing the front wheels to turn from the curb to the left. Then the car slowly wheeled out of the parking space and into the middle of the hill. While moving down the road, it was in "reverse" and the motor being "loose", kept the speed at about 10 miles per hour. Then seeing a parking spot open to its right, it turned and drove over the curb, through the space, and into a tree. When I got in, the car was still in reverse. I put it in "neutral", turned on the ignition, placed it in "drive", and drove away.

As instructed, I appeared before a judge. He asked me my name and occupation. Upon realizing I was a teacher, he told me that the fine for the offense was a minimum of 300 dollars. But being a teacher and since there had been no property damage or humans hurt, he said my fine would be $50.00. And with a promise that, at my earliest convenience, I would get the brakes fixed, he excused me, and I left.

Within the Week, I got the breaks fixed but at night before retiring, I always looked out the window at my parked 1948 red chevy just to make sure that it had not decided on its own, to venture out into the night, under its own power, to cause another mobile incident.

Made in the USA
Middletown, DE
05 January 2023

20403426R00015